99 EMBARASSING

DAD JOKES

I spent a lot of time, money, and effort childproofing my house... but the kids still get in.

My wife said I was immature. So I told her to get out of my fort.

What do sprinters eat before a race? Nothing, they fast!

Did you hear about the
restaurant on the moon?
Great food, no atmosphere!

Did you hear the rumor about butter? Well, I'm not going to spread it!

Why is Peter Pan
always flying?

He neverlands!

After an unsuccessful harvest, why did the farmer decide to try a career in music? Because he had a ton of sick beets.

What do you call a sad cup of coffee? Depresso.

My dog used to chase people on a scooter a lot. It got so bad we had to take his scooter away.

After dinner, my wife asked
if I could clear the table.
I needed a running start,
but I made it!

I know a lot of jokes about retired people but none of them work!

I hate it when people say age is only a number. Age is clearly a word.

Which days are the strongest? Saturday and Sunday. The rest are weekdays.

My doctor told me I was going deaf. The news was hard for me to hear.

I'm addicted to collecting vintage Beatles albums.

I need Help!

What's brown and sticky?

A stick.

My wife asked me to stop singing "Wonderwall" to her.
I said maybe...

Why do some couples go to the gym? Because they want their relationship to work out.

My boss told me to have a good day, so I went home.

When does a joke become a "dad joke?"
When it becomes apparent.

I was going to tell a time-traveling joke, but you guys didn't like it.

What did the
accountant say while
auditing a document?
This is taxing.

Why do melons have
weddings?
Because they cantaloupe.

Want to hear a joke about construction?
I'm still working on it.

If a child refuses to nap,
are they guilty of resisting
a rest?

I tell dad jokes, but I don't have any kids.
I'm a faux pa.

Why do dads feel the need to tell such bad jokes? They just want to help you become a groan up.

RIP boiled water—
you will be mist.

What does a house wear?
Address.

Why couldn't the bicycle stand up by itself? It was two-tired.

I'm so good at sleeping,
I can do it with my eyes
closed.

People are usually shocked that I have a Police record. But I love their greatest hits!

I like telling Dad jokes...
sometimes he laughs.

How do you weigh a millennial?

In Instagrams.

What does a baby computer call his father?

Data.

What's the difference between a well-dressed man on a unicycle and a poorly-dressed man on a bicycle? Attire.

My hotel tried to charge me ten dollars extra for air conditioning.
That wasn't cool.

Wanna hear a joke about paper? Nevermind. It's tearable.

I don't trust stairs.
They're always up to
something.

Imagine if you walked into a bar and there was a long line of people waiting to take a swing at you. That's the punch line.

What's an astronaut's favorite
part of the computer?

The Space Bar.

I was playing chess with my friend and he said, "Let's make this interesting." So we stopped playing chess.

Someone complimented my parking today!
They left a sweet note on my windshield that said "parking fine."

"Cop: I'm arresting you for downloading the entire Wikipedia."

Man: "Wait! I can explain everything!"

Not to brag but I made six figures last year. I was also named worst employee at the toy factory.

My friend claims he glued himself to his autobiography. I don't believe him, but that's his story and he's sticking to it.

A century ago, two brothers decided it was possible to fly. And as you can see, they were Wright.

I'm reading a horror story in braille. Something bad is going to happen, I can just feel it.

When I die, I want to be cremated. It's my last chance to have a smokin' hot body.

What's the best thing about living in Switzerland?
I don't know, but the flag is a big plus.

I always knock on the fridge door before opening it, just in case there's a salad dressing.

I tried to start a professional hide and seek team, but it didn't work out. Turns out, good players are hard to find.

As I get older, I remember all the people I lost along the way. Maybe a career as a tour guide was not the right choice.

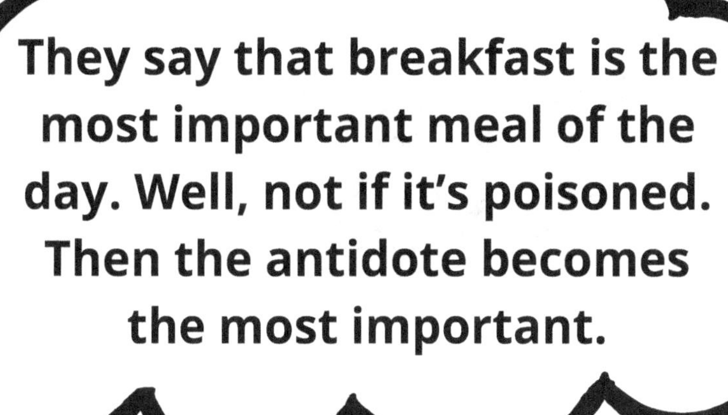

They say that breakfast is the most important meal of the day. Well, not if it's poisoned. Then the antidote becomes the most important.

In my free time, I like to help blind people.

Verb, not adjective.

What do you call bears
with no ears? B.

My wife told me she didn't understand cloning. I told her, "That makes two of us."

When I see the names of lovers engraved on a tree, I don't find it cute or romantic. I find it weird how many people take knives with them on dates.

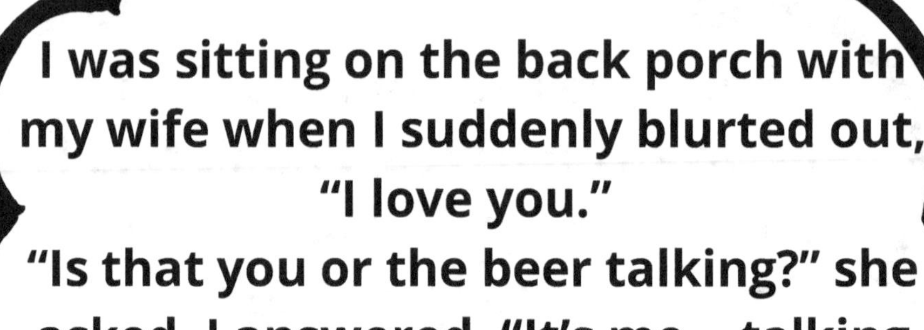

I was sitting on the back porch with my wife when I suddenly blurted out, "I love you."
"Is that you or the beer talking?" she asked. I answered, "It's me... talking to my beer."

"Siri," I asked my phone, "why am I so bad with women?" She responded, "I'm Bixby, you moron."

Marriage involves three rings: The engagement ring, the wedding ring, and the suffer-ring.

"Dad, can you explain to me what a solar eclipse is?"

No sun.

What did the buffalo say to his son when he dropped him off at school?

Bison.

A son tells his father, "I have an imaginary girlfriend." The father sighs and says, "You know, you could do better." "Thanks Dad," the son says. "That means a lot." The father shakes his head and goes, "I was talking to your girlfriend."

Yesterday, I was washing the car with my son. He said, "Dad, can't you just use a sponge?"

I tried to explain to my 4-year-old son that it's perfectly normal to accidentally poop your pants. But he's still making fun of me.

I wasn't close to my father when he died. Which is lucky because he stepped on a landmine.

Try the seafood diet.
You see food, then
you eat it.

You can't trust atoms.
They make up everything!

What did the police officer
say to her belly button?
You're under a vest!

I was wondering why the frisbee kept getting bigger and bigger.
Then it hit me.

I talk to myself because sometimes I just need expert advice.

I could tell a joke about pizza,
but it's a little cheesy.

I had to sell my vacuum cleaner. All it was doing was gathering dust.

"I'll call you later."
Don't call me later, call me Dad.

What's a sea monster's
favorite lunch?

Fish and ships.

Have you heard how popular
the local cemetery is?

People are just dying to get in.

Why do skeletons stay so calm?

Because nothing gets under their skin.

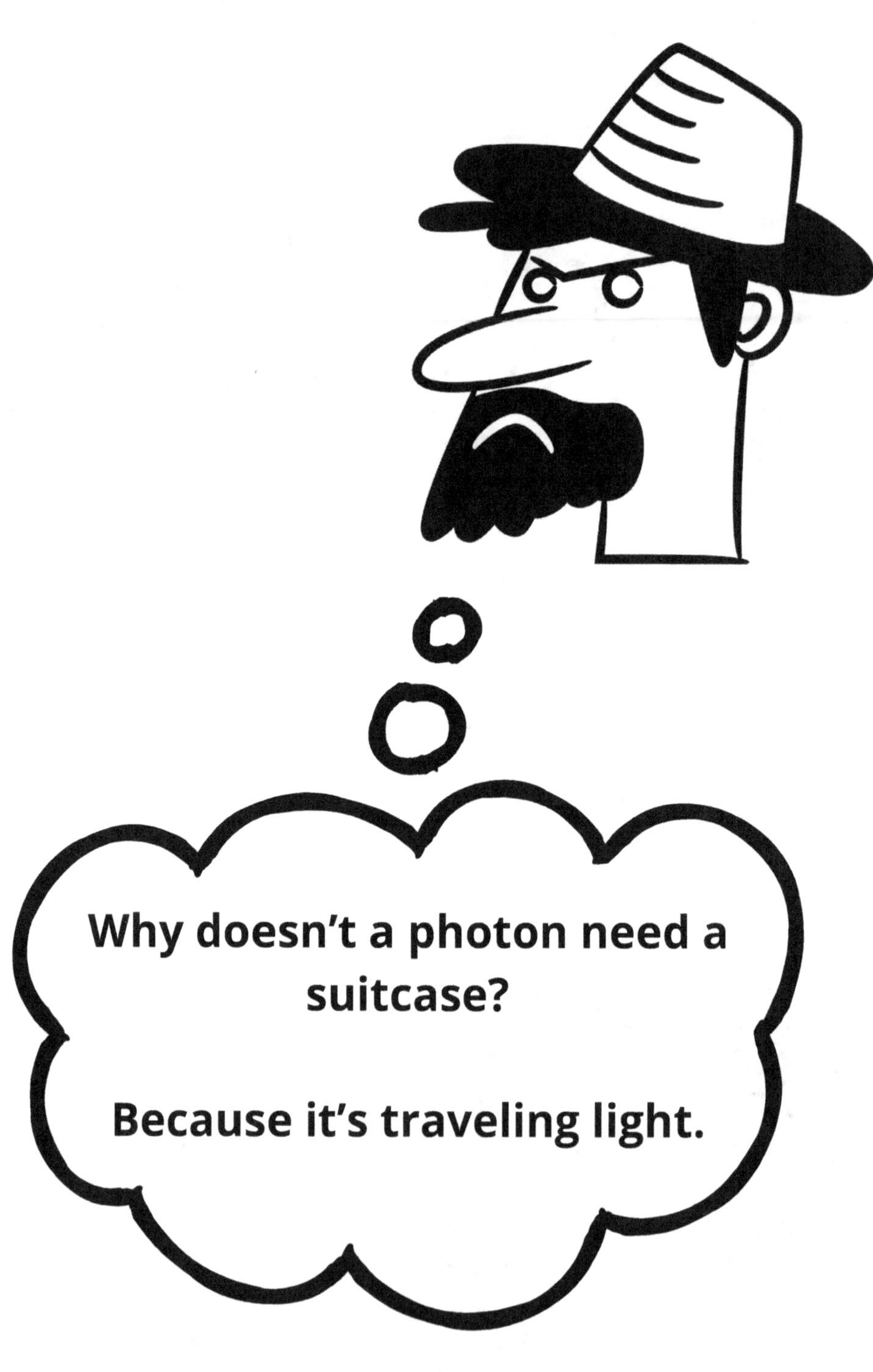
Why doesn't a photon need a suitcase?

Because it's traveling light.

What do you call a fish with four eyes?

Fiiiish!

What do you get when you coddle a cow?

Spoiled milk.

Did you ever notice ants don't get sick?

They're full of anty-bodies.

Last night my wife and I watched two DVDs back to back. Luckily I was the one facing the TV.

A sandwich walks into a bar. The barman says: 'sorry we don't serve food here'

What do you call a man with
a rubber toe?

Roberto!

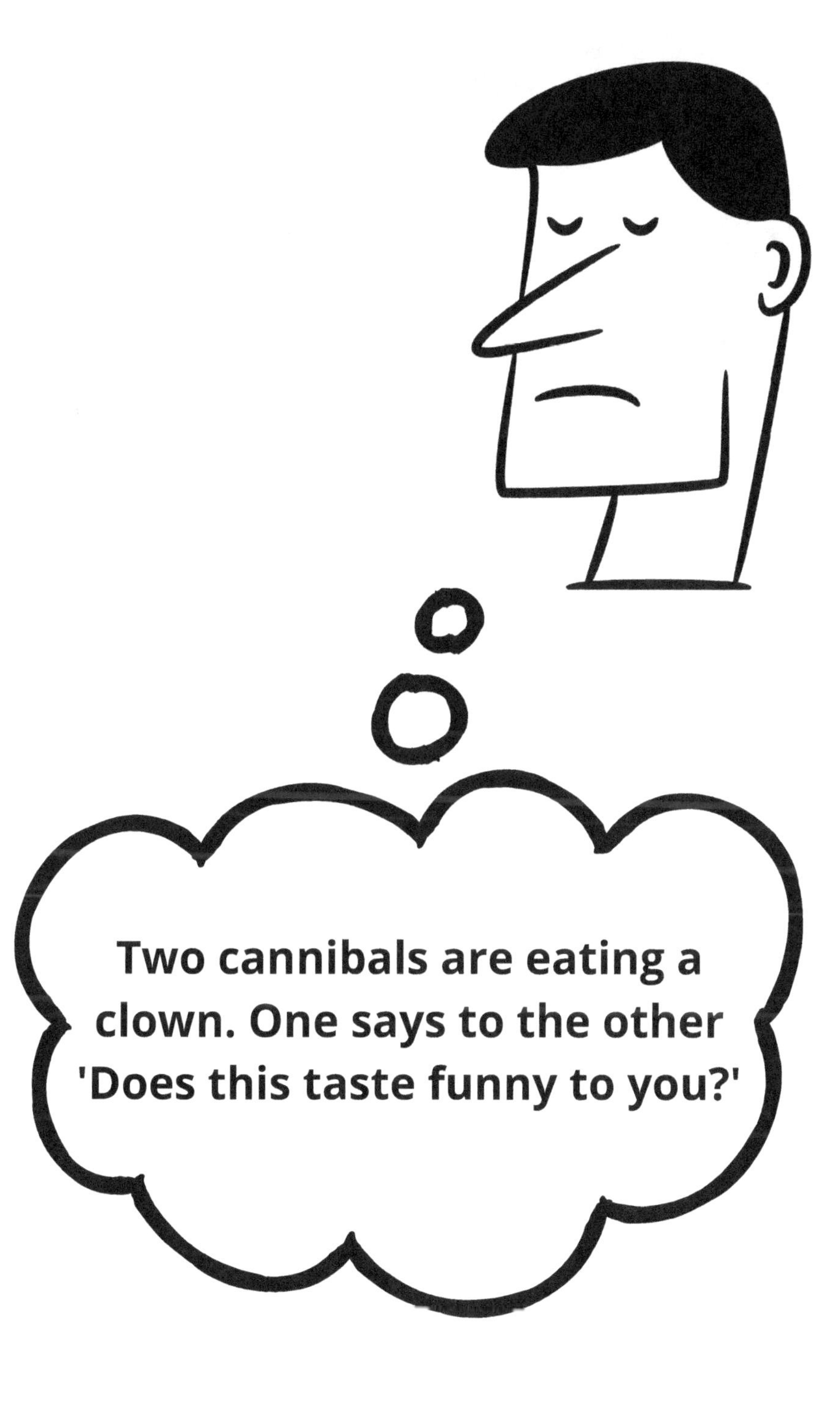
Two cannibals are eating a clown. One says to the other 'Does this taste funny to you?'

I remember the first time I saw a universal remote control.
I thought to myself 'well this changes everything'.

Did you hear about the kidnapping at school.
It's ok he woke up.

England doesn't have a kidney bank. But it does have a Liverpool.

I'd tell you a chemistry joke but I know I wouldn't get a reaction.

What did the late tomato
say to the other tomatoes?
Don't worry I'll ketchup.

Can I watch TV?
Yes, but don't
turn it on.

I'm reading a book about anti-gravity. It's impossible to put down.

What did the mountain climber
name his son?

Cliff.

Why don't crabs give to charity? Because they're shellfish.

Why is grass so dangerous?
Because it's full of blades.

What did the drummer
call his twin daughters?
Anna one, Anna two...

What's a bad wizard's
favorite computer program?

Spell-check.

I was just reminiscing about the beautiful herb garden I had when I was growing up. Good thymes.

www.ingramcontent.com/pod-product-compliance
Lightning Source LLC
Chambersburg PA
CBHW061338140726
47997CB00003B/1014